HOPE
for the
HOPELESS

presented to Matt + Beth
may God bless each of you.

by
Robert Aheron

Robert Aheron

Published by:

Empire Publishing, Inc.
(inside the House of Stars building on Highway 220)
PO Box 717
Madison, NC 27025-0717
Phone: 336-427-5850 • Fax: 336-427-7372
www.empirepublishinginc.com

Library of Congress Control Number: 2005935230
ISBN Number: 978-0-944019-46-7

Published and printed in the United States of America
1 2 3 4 5 6 7 8 9 10

CONTENTS

ACKNOWLEDGMENTS

First, I would like to thank God for His guidance and direction in my life and in the production of this book. I am greatly appreciative of my wife, Virginia, for her never-ending love and support. Special credit goes to my son, Daryl, and my friend, Martha Knight, for their assistance in writing and re-writing my manuscript. Lastly, I would like to thank Don, Rhonda and Doneen at Empire Publishing for their expertise and assistance in making my dream a reality.

My son, Daryl Aheron.

PREFACE

Hopefully you will find the hope that I have found as you read this book. The primary objective is that someone will be encouraged to look beyond themselves in a positive way and realize that if Robert Aheron overcame a very difficult beginning in life, you can also do it. The only way to make you aware of just how far the Lord has brought me (and He can do the same for anyone that puts his trust, faith or hope in Him) is to share with you some of my past, as difficult as that is. By using only a few names, I trust that I will not offend anyone

Please understand that I do not think I have arrived, but thank God I'm not what I used to be or could have been. This is to give Him all the credit for what He has done for me and through me to reach the achievements in my life. Any failure has been because of my disobedience and rebellion toward Him.

Jeremiah 17:7 "Blessed *is* the man that trusteth in the LORD, and whose **hope** the LORD is."

Romans 8:24-25 "For we are saved by **hope**: but **hope** that is seen is not **hope**: for what a man seeth, why doth he yet **hope** for?
25 But if we **hope** for that we see not, *then* do we with patience wait for *it*."

1 Corinthians 15:19 "If in this life only we have **hope** in Christ, we are of all men most miserable."

1 Peter 1:3 "Blessed *be* the God and Father of our Lord Jesus Christ, which according to his abundant mercy hath begotten us again unto a lively **hope** by the resurrection of Jesus Christ from the dead,"

Hebrews 11:1 "Now faith is the substance of things **hoped** for, the evidence of things not seen."

7

Chapter 1

In the Beginning

With the encouragement of several people who want me to write a book and after thinking about the help it will hopefully be to someone who has no hope, here I go. If only one hopeless person finds hope, it will be worth it.

The early part of my life is very difficult to talk about, not only because of the hurt but also because of the bitterness that was created within my heart. Let me say here that the bitterness has been replaced with the love that only God can give. When He changes our heart through His saving grace, He forgives our sin and helps us forgive others.

I was born into a dirt-poor farming family back in 1934 when times were bad, right after the Depression. My mother was sick with cancer and died when I was 27 months old, and my Father was drinking when he came to my mother's grave as she was

Ida D. Aheron (Mom)

Joe H. Aheron (Dad)

being buried. These tragedies started many years of hopelessness for me.

Much of my father's failure to keep our family together probably was of his own making. It could have been partly because he had been married twice before his marriage to my mother. His first marriage produced eight children, and that wife died, leaving him with those to raise. Then he remarried and had one son before he separated from his second wife; his third marriage produced Willie, Anne, Jimmy, and me. My mother being sick with cancer and dying so soon after my birth could have caused him to turn to drink. Maybe his children by his first wife turned against him, but whatever the cause, my mother's family did not like my father either. Once mother was dead, they had to decide what to do with the four of us children. We do remember that one of mother's sisters was a very caring and loving person who took care of me much of the time that mother was sick, but she was unable to care for all of us.

My mother's brothers and sisters decided to carry Willie, Anne, Jimmy and me to the home of one of our half brothers. He and his family were not there when we arrived. We were left on their porch and told to stay until they returned. Well when they returned, there were my half-brother, his wife and eight children of their own. Needless to say, we did not know what to expect, and neither did they; of course we were unwanted. Their family was large enough already. My half-brother and his wife did take us in and provided a place to eat and sleep until they could come up with an idea of what to do with us. And even until this day, I am grateful for that. They got Willie a place with another one of our half brothers, and Jimmy also went to live with one. Anne and I were able to stay there with them for a while. Having Anne with me was very important for me. It seemed that she was all I had.

A few things I remember while living there were a mad dog loose in the neighborhood and the police coming to take care of it down near the out john. Also, my nephew hit me in the head with his hammer and it bled, but the blame was mine because we were not to play with his things. Of course I was punished. Another thing that I recall is that we all carried water to the house from a pump down the street.

On Christmas Eve that year, the men at the local YMCA brought Anne and me a gift each. We had already gone to bed, but they were persistent that we get up and play with the train for me and the crystal for Anne. After a short time, the men left and we went back to bed. The next morning, the train was given to my nephew and the crystal to my niece. I received ten red switches instead, and of course they were worn out on me, one at a time until they were all gone.

Later my siblings and I were carried to the Rockingham County Home. But at least all of us were together again. We understood that there was a kind and wealthy lady who wanted to take us and keep all of us together. But somebody decided that would be too good for us; we did not deserve such kindness or good fortune. We were disliked so very much. And of course my question for many years was what had we done to deserve such treatment? We did not choose the situation we were in. There must have been a lot of hard feelings toward my dad and mom. We do not know any one person, rich, poor, black, white, who has anything to do with where, when, or to whom they are born. Only by the Grace of God are we who we are. We have nothing to do with it. So don't get so high and mighty about what you have; you did nothing to get it or to deserve whatever you have.

At the County Home, things were okay as long as Willie, Anne, Jimmy and I were together. But after a short time, the half brother and wife who previously had kept Jimmy came and took him with them – he stayed with them until he married. Willie was the next to leave, to work for a widow lady, and he stayed with her until he joined the Armed Services, Airborne Division.

Things were terrible for young children at the County Home. Most of the people were old, blind, and yes, crazy. White and black people were there. So with only Anne there to turn to, she became my only hope, more like a mother, sometimes like a cat carrying a kitten. During school season, when she walked to school, I would go to the corner of the fence that surrounded the County Home and watch her until she went out of sight. Then when she came home from school, she would see me at the same place waiting for her to return. She was all I had.

This is the County Home, as it looked during the time I lived there.

Chapter 2

Too Young to Understand

One day while at the County Home, my dad and Rev. William Gordon came to see Anne and me. They carried us down into a room and talked to us about accepting the Lord. I was only about 4 years of age, and I did not understand what they were talking about. So Anne told me to just say yes, but not understanding, my answer was no. I never did understand and kept telling Anne that I didn't. Dad and preacher Gordon left. They meant well, but I was too young to understand, and so my answer was no. Sure there was concern for us. There were church groups that came and sang songs like "Amazing Grace," "The Old Rugged Cross," "Blessed Assurance," and others. They would preach, but most of the time there were other things for me to do. That stuff was for those old folks – not me. Sure I can remember those songs along with so much more. God surely gave me a memory. I have not forgotten much of anything that has happened during my life, even the very early part of it.

Then Anne was taken away; oh, my life could have ended that day. All of my hope just went away, and I was so alone with no one to turn to. Sometimes Crazy Eller would catch me in the bathroom, and she would try to flush me down the commode. Sometimes in the middle of the night when everyone else was asleep, she would use a broom handle and run and scream at the top of her voice, dragging that broom handle across the water radiators that ran under the windows for heat in that large room.

There were at least eight or ten of us in there. It would scare me to my wits' end. I could feel my body rise straight up off the bed, scared stiff.

Well, the trustee prisoners who helped to look after the grounds and stock (cows, pigs and horses) and to raise the food that fed all of us at the County Home and the adjoining prison were the ones I turned to for friendship. Some of them took a liking to me, and as you may expect, some were good to me, but others were very mean. One time that I would like to forget was when two men coaxed me into a building and raped me. Oh I felt so awful and violated. I could not tell anyone; I was afraid to. The prisoners used and abused me in so many ways; it is still hard to talk about. They taught me so much meanness, words that only a few sailors would say.

Across the road from the County Home was a graveyard where several of the old folks who had died without family were buried with only rocks to mark the graves. Their burials were about the only time we were able to get out of the gates of the County Home.

After staying there for three years and seven months, when school was about to start for me, Mrs. Wilson, the head of the children's welfare department, came and carried me to a family. They already had a boy named Johnny, so they had to call me by my middle name, Robert. These people that I went to live with were very proper and good people and somewhat religious, which was hard for me to get used to. My vocabulary, being what it had become, sure got me into a lot of trouble with this new family. They tried to correct me and my language many times by trying to beat it out of me. They would pass me from one to the other, beating me with a switch and sometimes a razor strap. The blood would run down my legs, and if I had shoes on, into my shoes. Oh yes, I tried to clean up my speech, but I would say the wrong thing again, and the whipping just got worse. They would tell me not to talk like that in front of those other children, but I did not know any better. It was very difficult.

The state paid the family one dollar a day to keep us, and there were three other children that they were keeping at that time, one boy and two girls, all older than me. And, of course, you know who got the blame for anything they did wrong. They learned that quickly.

These people did teach me a lot, and they were good people, but it took us a long time to get used to each other. They were determined to help me with my language, and they did. At school my grades were very good for the three and half years that I was there. The other children helped me with my schoolwork, and with them being older, it made it easier to learn. We were only permitted to use the indoor bathroom when we were sick. We took our baths in a wash tub, not in the regular bathtub. But as I look back now, I'm very thankful for that family. I worked hard as a child. Each of us had chores to do, and I learned to work on a farm.

Then Mrs. Wilson came and carried me to another family when I was about nine and a half years old. I stayed there only a few days. They could not stand me; I was too mean to be around their two small children. I had not received all of my books until the morning that Mrs. Wilson came to get me at school. She said, "John Robert, leave your books and come with me".

I had been told that my next place would be Jackson Training School (a home in North Carolina for delinquent boys), but Mrs. Wilson carried me and several others to Reidsville for physicals that were required by the state. And then she said that she would carry us by the drug store and buy us a piece of candy or ice cream. Well, instead of ice cream or candy, I wanted the nickel or dime. Oh yes, no doubt I had rather have the same as the other children, but I would do without so as to save the money – to the sum of two dollars and fifteen cents. I had it in a stud tobacco bag with a drawstring top. That and the clothes on my back, a white T-shirt and a pair of short pants were all of my possessions.

Chapter 3

A Home at Last?

After taking me to another place where the people decided they did not want me, Mrs. Wilson brought me to a Mr. and Mrs. Lawrence. I will never forget that day. He was sitting in a rocking chair in front of the window with a spittoon beside his chair. He had not shaven lately and had amber juice all over his chin. She was in bed sick. Three of his sons were sitting backwards in straight chairs around a wood heater asleep. When one of them woke up, he looked at me, and with a very mean, scratchy voice said, "My God boy, where did you come from?" Well, I was thinking, "What in this world have I gotten into now?" My feet were saying run, but I did not know where to run. It was a very gray day with misty rain in a different part of Rockingham County. I did not know what to say or do. Hopeless would not describe how I felt. This must be the end of the line for me. How could anything be any worse than this? Everywhere that they had taken me, all the people seemed to know where to put the blame for all the bad things that happened. I had to learn to live with that fact.

One day after getting settled in with a new school and these people, Mr. Lawrence told me to get an axe because we were going to haul some wood. We went into the woods, some distance over the hill from the house, and loaded the two-horse wagon with the wood. On the way back, I was driving the wagon when he said "Stop and tie the mules to that tree, get your axe, and come with me." Just a little ways down the hill to a gully, he began to pull back some branches and said to me, "Take your axe and hit that still." Well, I didn't know what to expect but did as I was told. When I hit that still, the mash came spewing out, and it smelled awful. Then a little later we did the same thing again to another liquor still just a short distance from the other one. Both of these belonged to his sons. We raised the crops, tobacco, corn, wheat, oats, garden, and neither one of his sons spoke to their father all during that time. If they had anything to say to him, they would have someone else to tell him. That was very sad. Oh, if I could have had the chance to see and talk to my dad, what a blessing that would have been. Their father had cut down the stills to keep them from getting caught by the law. Of course, it cost them a lot of money because sugar was rationed, as were many other products in the early 1940's during World War II. The year was 1944, and I was ten years old. These were very poor, hard working people trying to make a dollar bill any way they could. They were sharecroppers, giving one half of all they made to the owners of the land. It was a very hard life and very difficult to get by debt free from one year to the next. Many times there was nothing left over. Most of their equipment and furnishings were old because there never seemed to be enough money to buy anything new.

We even shared our help with others. Once while we were housing tobacco, one of Mr. Lawrence's sons hit me across the head with a tobacco stick, breaking the stick and knocking me out. He did this because I could not lift the tobacco up over the flue pipes that ran through the barn. That green tobacco was very heavy before being cured. Being very young and very tired from priming and handing leaves as it was strung on the stick, I just could not hold it up high enough to keep the tails off the flue pipes for such a long time. He did not care about that and did not understand. It was just another way to strike out at me. They did this many times over a period of years. They took a lot of their hate and frustrations out on me, sometimes hitting me with rocks, tree limbs, sticks, or whatever was handy.

Mr. and Mrs. Lawrence were good old people, but they had a

lot of bad health problems. They let me stay with them for several years. I looked after them in their sickness and worked very hard trying to make sure they had food, medicine, or whatever they needed.

When I was fourteen years old, Mr. Lawrence had a major surgery, and the doctors told him he could never work again. With his age and the operation being so severe, he could only do very light work. So doing the farm work and taking care of them became heavier on me. But working as I did helped to make me strong, and I loved to help those fine people all I could.

Mrs. Wilson came again. I was busting wood at the woodpile when she came. We cooked in an old wood cook stove and heated the house with wood heaters or sometimes with a fireplace, so it took a lot of wood. Mrs. Wilson spoke on her way into the house, and after being there a short time, she called for me to come inside and get my things. She said that the state required that we get a high school education, and I was going to be moved. When I got into the house, I stopped just inside the doorway. She repeated again that she had come to take me some place else. I told her that I wanted to stay and take care of Mr. and Mrs. Lawrence. I was not going anywhere else with her. I would choose my place to stay; if she tried to make me leave, I would go away, and they would never see me again. Mr. Lawrence rose up in his bed and told her to leave me with them, that I would do exactly what I said. He said, "If he tells you something, he will do it." I went back out and started busting wood again. On her way out Mrs. Wilson said, "John Robert, you take care of yourself". That was the last time I remember seeing her.

The next day I went to school and turned in my books. I was going to take care of those fine old people. Being in school only two or three days a week made it very difficult to maintain good grades. They needed much care, and trying to raise the crops that were needed to pay the bills would take a lot of time. Would I do this over again, giving up my education and being a caregiver at my young age? Yes, there was something inside of me that would not let me walk away from these folks. They had become such a stable source in my life and were as good to me as they could be.

The hours were long as I was getting up sometimes at 3:30 a.m. and going to bed late. We make choices all through life, and I made this one because someone needed me. Cooking their food and sometimes sitting beside their bed and spoon feeding each of them never became a burden. To buy groceries, medicine, and whatever else they needed gave me a sense of being helpful and special for someone else. I did not have much time for myself because the work was very hard. I primed tobacco, cut logs, mowed yards, helped to build barns, and worked at a sawmill just to make enough money to buy food, medicine or whatever was needed. But God has surely blessed me for doing this.

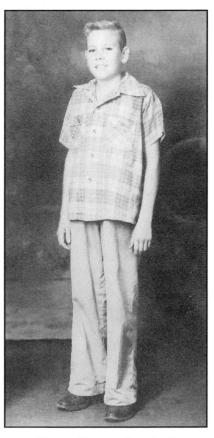

I still love to work even until this day. Hard work is good for us; I never have gotten anything except through hard work. It has been a way of life. God says let a man earn his living by the sweat of his brow. I don't believe in "by hook or by crook", taking advantage of others. I could have made tons of money if money had been my motivation. I have turned down much more money, power, and prestige than I have received. But everything has been earned with a clear conscious; I can sleep well at night because of treating others fairly. God will take care of us

Jimmy Aheron (brother)

Here I am wearing one of the sweaters given to me by my siblings.

if only we will obey Him and His Word. Money or things will not bring happiness.

After several years of not seeing my two brothers and sister, they came to see me at Mr. Lawrence's. Each one got me a Christmas gift. As I opened each gift, they started looking at each other and smiling. Each one of them had me a sweater, all a different color and style. The gifts were great, but just seeing them and being with each of them was far greater to me than any gift could ever be. Please remember they did not live with each other but had gotten together just to bring me Christmas gifts.

We began seeing each other as often as possible. Willie had gotten his driver's license. I was able to attend each of my brothers' weddings. I was also able to visit my sister some. We visited each other and shared our love, appreciation, and respect. Sure, each of us would have a different story to tell because each one was raised so differently. They never got into the mischief and meanness that I did. They kept their lives clean and proper and

Willie Aheron (brother)

did very well in the end.

Our get-togethers were what I would call quality time together. And a few times (before our daddy died at a ripe old age) we all were together on special occasions. I understand that Dad helped build the Rock Church in Spray. He and our half-brothers hauled many of the rocks in that church (before we were born of course). And each day at a certain time during World War II, Dad would ring the bell so that people would stop and pray,

Anne Aheron Thacker (sister)

not just for our brother Willie, but for all the troops and our country. So our dad did not die as a drunk but died with a testimony that he

The inside of the Rock Church that my father helped build.

loved and served God. Thanks be unto my Lord.

When I was sixteen years old, a man asked me to come and stay with him to help with a large farm. He said that when he died, the farm would be mine. But I could not leave Mr. and Mrs. Lawrence. They needed me. After he died, that farm was worth over six million dollars. Have I thought about all that wealth? Sure I have, but I know that what was done was the right thing to do. God surely blessed me for my choices.

Of course, the bitterness was still in my heart. People looked down on me, abused, mistreated, and used me as a scapegoat. That made me tough, mean, and strong. I sort of got used to that, but it still hurt. People would sic their dogs on me; I've been shot at, cursed, hated – that just made me worse.

One day when I was sixteen, one of Mr. Lawrence's sons came over drunk, as he had done several times before. He started cursing and belittling Mrs. Lawrence who was not his real mother. When I came in, I knew this had to stop. I was tired and fed up with such action toward her. I told him to leave her alone because she had cooked and washed his clothes and had not done anything against him. He turned on me, but that did not work. That was the last time he ever did that to her or to me.

Exterior of Rock Church (St. Luke's Episcopal).

Chapter 4

Honky-Tonk Robert

As I got older, the meaner and wilder I became. At night I would drink and honky-tonk around. My neighbor nicknamed me Honky-Tonk, and of course I tried to live up to that. On the weekends I went to the honky-tonks, dance halls, or wherever the fights or mischief were. There seemed no hope of ever making anything out of my life. Most people without any purpose in life end up dead, in prison, or on the streets – which easily could have happened to me had it not been for the Grace of God.

One Christmas Eve my date and I had started to a dance, but first she wanted to go to see her little brother who was in a church Christmas play. We went in and sat near the back of the church. A young lady that I knew from school a few years back asked us to go Christmas caroling with them after the play. My date did not want to go, but I told the young lady that I would go if she would ride with me. She said she would, and I carried her home. After that we began dating. She was different from the other girls I had dated. She would not go to the dance hall, movies, or places that I wanted to go. She always wanted to go to church or a gospel singing. Well, I wanted to be with her, and I fell in love for the first time with someone very special. We dated for over two months, and one Saturday night after church, as I left her at her door, she told me that she was going to be praying for me. I could not get away from that statement. No one had ever cared enough for me to pray for me. I had been leaving my girl's house and going by the dance hall every Saturday night for a long time, but now I told the guys that I was going home early. Many Saturday nights we had stayed out all night drinking, fighting, and carousing around or doing whatever meanness we could get into. I was one of the ringleaders, but that night I was home about 12:30 a.m. I went to bed and tried to sleep, but sleep was replaced with my past remembrances. **It made me aware of how helpless and hopeless my life really was** without any of my real family around. I had no REAL friends, just the ones with whom I drank and honky-tonked. I had very little education to draw from, and no one except this one lady really cared.

The next day was Sunday, March 8, 1953. Virginia and I met at church for the morning worship service and spent the afternoon together. Then, of course, we went to church that night, and nothing would do for her but to sit near the front – the fourth row from the front on the left side next to the isle.

So the preacher preached; it appeared that someone had told him all about me, for his eyes seemed to fall on me most of the time. As the invitation song was sung ("Just As I Am"), my feet moved right into the center isle. And on my knees at that church altar that night, **I gave my heart and life to Jesus Christ,** and He came into my unworthy heart and soul. **He saved me from my sin and from myself. Thanks be unto His marvelous Grace as I repented of my sins.**

That night in my front pant pocket was a switch blade knife and a set of dice. In my shirt pocket was a deck of cards. Under the seat of my car were a two-foot-long chain and a bottle of whiskey. They were the things that I liked to use in my fighting, drinking, and gambling. It was just a way of life to me.

Those things are not needed anymore. God so wonderfully took all of that away and gave me something much better. I have not been the same since that night; He turned me completely around.

Jeremiah 17:7 *"Blessed is the man that trusteth in the LORD, and whose **hope** the LORD is."*

I was headed for Hell and destruction, and may I say, very quickly; now I am headed to Heaven **with such hope, peace, and love.** I cannot get over the difference the Lord makes, nor do I want to; it just gets sweeter and better each day.

Robert and Virginia

Romans 8:24 *"For **we are** saved by hope: but hope that is seen is not hope: for what a man seeth, why doth he yet hope for?"*

Oh, I know that I am not all that I should and could be, and I have failed my Lord in so many ways. Many times I have been disobedient and rebellious, but thank God He is patient and merciful as He shapes me into what He wants me to be. So thanks be unto Him again, this old sinner is not what he used to be – praise His precious name.

I Peter 1:13 *"Blessed be the God and Father of our Lord Jesus Christ, which according to his abundant mercy hath begotten us again unto a **lively hope** by the resurrection of Jesus Christ from the dead,"*

Virginia and I got married November 26, 1953. Now we

Johnny, Daryl, and Steve

24

have been married over fifty-one years. She still is the love of my life, but not all of the fifty-one years have been a bed of roses; however, it sure beats the tar out of the first nineteen years of my life. We have been so wonderfully blessed. We have three fine sons and three fine grandsons and a great granddaughter.

Joey (grandson)

Johnny, our oldest, is a very highly skilled, talented person with great work ethics. He was a very good student in school and such a very good athlete in all sports, with many achievements and medals. Now he is one of the best builders we know and has his licenses for realty and brokerage. Johnny is a wonderful, caring person who treats others as he would want to be treated. Johnny and Carolyn have been married for over 30 years and have provided us with two fine grandsons – Joey and Timmy. Joey has provided us with Hailey, our great granddaughter.

Timmy (grandson)

Daryl, our middle son, is so very smart and is a loving, dedicated Christian. He is very trustworthy, he does a lot of missionary work, and he has written a book (Faith In Christ). He is also a Gideon, placing God's Holy Word around the world. Daryl has a very technical mind; he worked in Sandia National Laboratories

Justice (grandson)

(where weapons systems are designed) for eleven years. He knows a lot about so many things. What a blessing he is to us. Daryl and Hsiao-Wei have been married for over 17 years.

Steven, our youngest, has such great hand-eye coordination that he can do most anything with his hands. He was a very good athlete all through school and college. He has his realty, brokerage, and auctioneering licenses. Steven can do about anything he puts his mind to do. What a bundle of joy. Steven and Beth Anne have been married over 15 years and have provided us with our other grandson, Justice.

So the **hopelessness** that once was mine is now all gone; it has been replaced with the Blessed Hope found only in and through the Lord Jesus Christ.

Titus 2:13 *"Looking for that blessed hope, and glorious appearing of the great God and our Saviour Jesus Christ;"*

The Holy Spirit of God came into my heart and replaced the hate and bitterness with His love and peace beyond words.

Hailey (great-granddaughter)

26

I Corinthians 15:19 *"If in this life only we have **hope** in Christ, we are of all men most miserable."*

I think it would be impossible for God the Creator of Heaven and earth and all within to come into a person's heart and not make a big difference.

Again to those that feel that there is **no hope, there is hope** if we will only look beyond ourselves and others and unto the right source. **You can find hope in my Savior Jesus Christ.** He wants to be your Savior, Lord, and friend. God gave His only begotten son, and His son gave Himself on Calvary for you and for all that will trust (have faith) and accept Him as Savior.

Hebrews 11:1 *"Now faith is the substance of things hoped for, the evidence of things not seen."*

My family: Back Row (L-R) Steven, Robert, Virginia, Johnny. Middle: Beth Ann, Hsiao-Wei, Leslie, Carolyn. Front Row: Timmy, Justice, Joey. Not Pictured: Daryl.

Chapter 5

Showers of Blessings

God has wonderfully blessed my life in so many ways. Not only has He given me a fine wife and family, but He has provided me a good church in which to work and serve Him. He allowed me to teach Sunday school for many years and to be Sunday school superintendent and deacon. He has given me opportunities to conduct cottage prayer meetings in many homes and to lead and direct the youth, seeing many come to know my Lord as their Lord. Oh, the list of blessings in service goes on.

The Lord has provided me many opportunities through jobs and the people I have come in contact with along the way. As I remember back to the time when I was still living with Mr. & Mrs. Lawrence, I recall that I worked for three winters at Cone Mills at the White Oak Plant as a spare hand on second shift. A spare hand was one that did any job in the plant when someone was absent that day. We had to learn each job and then be able to do the many different jobs in the plant. As you may know, farming was always an ongoing learning process. I learned much about life, how to manage the stock and the land, how to sow and reap, and the weather always played a part in it. Knowing how to adjust quickly at times to the changing weather helped me learn to adjust to the different jobs readily.

Being fast, strong, and able to apply the experiences on the farm and having the ability to do things in the quickest and best possible way helped me to achieve much. So when the opportunity came at Blue Bell, starting at the very lowest paying job offered, we were able to use all the above to quickly move upward. Most all the jobs in the Cutting Department were on production work. That was just dandy with me; I could use my speed, strength, and quickness to my advantage. It did not take long before we were making the highest units – that's what we were paid by. Each unit was considered one minute of workload. Sixty units an hour were considered average.

They kept moving me up as we (Often, I use the word "we" to mean "the Lord and me," as I am nothing without Him.) were able to master each job: spreading cloth, assembling parts of cut work, cutting the cloth into garments to be sewn. For two straight years the division manager brought my W-2 Form (this shows the amount that we made during the entire year to file taxes for) and presented it to me for being the highest paid production worker in the entire company.

Working hard, finding ways to do things better, turning these suggestions into the suggestion box, and receiving rewards for each one that they could use helped me tremendously toward future positions.

The company just could not move me up fast enough to suit them. They wanted me in a management position. As an assistant manager in the cutting department on first shift, I also supervised the entire second shift in cutting, pressing, receiving, and parts. All of this was a good learning experience. People throughout the building respected me so much as we worked together getting the job done. When we would have a little bottleneck, all of us would jump in and clear it out so that everything would run smoothly. They liked the teamwork approach. As workers would ask for my help, they knew we could do whatever was needed together. They asked me questions about how they could improve on their job; we were always willing to help. Thanks again to my Lord, the answers seemed to come easily.

At thirty years of age it was time for me to get my GED Diploma. After taking some night classes, we passed the GED in the top 5% nationwide. Only God could have given me the knowledge and understanding to do this after being out of school for sixteen years.

The company was pleased when the GED was added to my file. They received a letter from Dr. Love at UNCG. What that letter contained we do not know, but they surely took notice to the achievement, especially at my age. They continued to find new places to use me. Being able to work in the Research and Development Department was a great way to use my creative ideas.

The jobs just kept opening up, one after the other, and I had to make choices very fast. Some jobs offered to me were easy to say no to, while some were more difficult to decide about.

The company was in the process of building a large new plant in Wilson, North Carolina, and my boss wanted me to run the cutting department once the new plant was finished. They put me in a training program that carried me through many departments for a two-week stay in each department. Once I came to the pattern department, things changed. After the first week there, I was called in and asked how I liked this type of work. I found it different, very interesting, and very creative. The head of this department wanted to know if I would be interested in staying a while longer; of course I would have to ask my boss about staying some time longer. He said, "Yes, but don't get too comfortable." He had been very good to me, and he stated that he didn't want to lose me; he also reminded me of the goals he had for me. After the second week, the head of the pattern department again called me into his office and made me aware that Mr. C.T. Yarber, the only head pattern designer for the company for nearly twenty-eight years, was to retire in two years, and he was looking for a replacement to train. I never imagined that they would look toward an uneducated person such as me, but they did.

The department head wanted me to be the person to replace Mr. Yarber. He liked what I did, the way I worked, and the way I conducted myself during the training period. I told him it would have to be approved by my boss, so he contacted my boss and discussed the situation. My boss reluctantly approved, stating that whatever I decided was okay and he only wanted what was best for me. My boss told me that I had his permission to spend more time in the pattern department until I could make up my mind about what was best for me. The decision was very hard because my boss had been so kind and good to me. Several weeks filled with lots of praying passed before I made my final decision. Remember, my expertise was in cutting, and my knowledge about pattern design only came by working with them in the cutting department and using the patterns to do so.

Well, after much prayer, the Lord just seemed to lead me into this area, and with a step of faith and an attempt to follow the guidance of my Lord, I accepted the position. As I look back, it was the correct move. The head of the pattern department and I sat down to discuss the new job, and I made sure that he understood my priorities in life: God first, family second, and job third. I told him I would give my job one hundred and ten percent as long as it did not take away from serving my Lord and taking care of my family. He understood and said that was what he was looking for in a replacement for Mr. Yarber.

Well, the way things worked out, surely God was totally with me; He gave me understanding in the pattern designing and making area. Mr. Yarber had told some of our co-workers that he would never train or teach anyone else how to do his job. He said that they would have to learn the hard way as he had done, but there again, only God could have changed his mind.

After a few weeks of training with Mr. Yarber, he taught me everything he knew and seemed to even go beyond himself, trying to be sure to cover every possible situation. So after two years of training and going to night classes, at his retirement, I was well equipped to take over as the master pattern maker and designer for Blue Bell, from toddlers, boys, girls, juniors, ladies, mens, in shirts, jackets, coats, jeans, pants, shorts, overalls, coveralls (lined and unlined), outerwear, swimwear, headwear, boots, gloves, whatever.

Being the one to give new employees their first two weeks of orientation training, I met people from all walks of life and other nations. Most had at least four years of college education, and we learned so much from each other.

The blessing always was mine because I was able to contribute to their progress in life by giving them encouragement as they began their new jobs. Hopefully I would help them somewhat to understand the things they would encounter later, and of course I would try to give some wisdom on how to handle the future. Being able to train over two hundred of these people surely contributed to my understanding of others. Each one of them was different, with different backgrounds and different individual ways of expressing themselves. Many of them were just out of college, and some were beginning a new job or career in another line of work. Whatever the situation, it was a challenging but a rewarding experience just to be able to touch so many in a very positive way. Thank God. With time there were many more that I had the privilege to train.

There were many challenges, but God always gave me the time and ability needed to get the job done. Sometimes we had to work through break, lunch, and many evenings to finish the projects.

Chapter 6

Brushing Shoulders with Celebrities

A big challenge early on was when we were asked to make and grade (grading is when you use one size pattern to make all the other sizes needed by increasing or reducing the measurements to achieve the proper fit) robes for the North Carolina Philharmonic Symphony Choir that travels all over the world. There were so many different sizes – large, small, tall, short – and each robe had to fit the same on each member. We finished the job on time; our seamstresses worked very hard helping us to finish by the scheduled time as we had promised. Thank the Lord. This task was over and beyond our regular work load, but again team work surely paid off.

What a blessing it was to be able to help others! I remember when the world's largest man was in town with the fair. He needed clothes, and we were asked to see what we could do for him. We went to the mobile unit where he lived and got measurements, designed a pattern for him, and one of the seamstresses sewed garments for him. We also made garments for two other fair employees: the largest lady and the tallest person. Handicapped individuals and hospitals, especially Duke Hospital, were recipients of our creative efforts. My name and the Blue Bell pattern department's name had gotten out, and people understood that we were willing to use our spare time to help others. Thank God we never turned anyone in need away. You must know that only God could give the understanding and the abilities we needed;

we were only vessels used by Him. Undeserving as we may have been, we received a plaque for going over and beyond the call of duty and contributing to team work.

Over the years the Lord blessed me with the opportunity to work with many celebrities such as Jim Shoulders, Speckled Brown, Jim Mahann from the Pro Rodeo Circuit, Lew Alcinder (Pro Basketball), Lee Trivino, Gary Player and family (Pro Golfers), Dale Earnhardt, Ricky Rudd, Jackie Stewart (Race Car Drivers), Jimmy Dean, B.J. Thomas, Willie Nelson and others (Music Artist Performers), and we even designed and made garments for President Ronald Reagan. Only God could have caused this to happen.

When Mr. L.K. Mann was the president and chief executive officer of Blue Bell, he called me into his office and asked me to become his right hand man. He wanted me to be a trouble shooter and to travel all over the world, finding problems and offering solutions on ways of fixing them. This request just blew me away; with over thirty thousand good employees to choose from, for him to choose me was just too much to comprehend. The idea of money, prestige, power, and world travel, caused my brain to say yes, but through many prayers, my heart would not let me take this position. I was afraid that maybe this new position would get my mind and heart set on myself, the material things of life, and the world. The fear of turning away from God caused me to say no to the position. I just couldn't get a peace of mind and heart about accepting the position. Several months later the same offer was made to me, and again I had to turn it down. Many times we are tempted and tried, but as we seek God's face and will for our lives, we can have peace if He leads us. We must be obedient unto Him and His leadership. We were able to come up with the right person for the position at my suggestion. That person was contacted and trained with me for six months. He took the position and eventually became a very wealthy person.

Then when Mr. L.K. Mann recommended me to teach evening

classes in pattern making and designing at UNCG for two nights each week (Tuesday & Thursday), again I was blown away. However, due to my busy schedule which required travel much of the time, I had to turn down the opportunity. It has been and still is very humbling to think of the opportunities the Lord has provided this old boy. You would think that we were as smart as some people think they are.

In 1986 the new president of Blue Bell, Mr. Ed Bauman, called and asked me to design and make a pattern for a pair of giant jeans to be presented to President Ronald Reagan. We would use the title "Crafted With Pride" in order to try and keep our textile jobs here in the United States. We had most of our employees all over America sign their names on the cloth donated by Burlington Industries. After the cloth was returned to me, we were able to make a pattern, cut the jean out, and sew it in our sample department with our seamstresses' help. We had the privilege of carrying it to the Capital in Washington, D.C. We presented it to N. C. Representative Howard Coble, Senator Jesse Helms, and Vice President George H.W. Bush. We draped that pair of giant

World's Largest Pair of Jeans—signed by more than 16,000 Blue Bell employees, these jeans measure 54 feet in length with a 35-foot waist. Over 2-1/2 miles of thread were used to sew the jeans out of 175 yards of denim. Each hip pocket can hold three adults.

jeans at the Capital Building steps, reaching from the top of the steps to the bottom, making it over four stories in length.

Never did we dream or even think someone would put my name in the *Guiness Book of World Records* because of this, but they did. The jeans were not made for this purpose; we were just trying to save jobs in the textile industry. We may have failed, but we surely got some people to pay attention, at least for a short time.

Here we are calculating the measurements needed for grading the other sizes at Blue Bell's pattern department.

Chapter 7

Retirement?

After retiring from Blue Bell with thirty-two years of service, I started my own consultant business. I was able to do a lot of good work for many large and small companies. The telephone would ring often with job offers to the tune of forty-three different companies, from East and West, North and South, and many told me to name my own price. It is very humbling to think that the Lord had provided me with such awesome experiences. People from Vogue, Simplicity, Sears, Gap, Izod, Perry Ellis, Levi Strauss and many others rated me as one of the top ten designers in the world. It was wonderful to have skills that so many companies wanted and needed, and they were willing to pay top dollar.

Thanks be unto my God, for He has certainly made all the difference in my life; **He has given me such hope,** not just for the moment but for the future. He not only is **my Savior**, but **my Lord** and Master, **my hope, my guide, my life.**

He has been so very good to me and my family. I could not and would not want to be without Him for even one second. He says He will never leave us or forsake us and will go with us even unto the end of the way, John 14:6 *"He is the way, the truth and the life."* God is the only way, and since He came into my heart, the way is so much better. **What hope is within.** He is the only truth; He never leads us wrong, Psalm 118:8 *"It is better to trust in the Lord, than to put your confidence in man."* Man will fail you, but God never fails. That is the truth. He is the only life. Well, if you are reading this book, you can plainly see what my life was like before Jesus Christ; it wasn't good in any way. **I was so hopeless,** but you can see and understand why I now say life is so good since coming to know Him.

God's Word teaches us how to live this new life. **"Do unto others as you would have them do unto to you"** (Refer to Matthew 7:12).

> Luke 6:38 *"Give, and it shall be given unto you; good measure, pressed down, and shaken together, and running over, shall men give into your bosom. For with the same measure that ye mete* [give] *withal it shall be measured to you again."* **You just cannot out give God.**

> II Corinthians 9:6-9 *"But this I say, he which soweth sparingly shall reap also sparingly, and he which soweth bountifully shall reap bountifully. Every man according as he purposeth in his heart, so let him give; not grudgingly or of necessity, for God loveth a cheerful giver, and God is able to make all grace abound toward you, that ye, always having all sufficiency in all things, may abound to every good work."*

Since He took control of our lives, we have not been too concerned about where we would sleep, what we would have to eat, or any other thing we might need. Everything has been supplied by my Lord. You know what He said about the lilies.

I know there are many people who just can't get enough money, land, or material things. We can honestly say that when we let God control our lives, these things have taken care of themselves. I know it takes money to live on, but the love of money is the root of all evil. Greed is such a terrible thing. Another thing that destroys many people is bitterness and jealousy; it eats from within to without. We just can't let these feelings stay within our hearts.

Thanks be unto my Lord. He not only took away the taste of whiskey, the love of fighting, playing poker, cursing, carousing and so many other things, but also the bitterness is gone. I must admit that it did take a while for me to forgive the many people who were so mean to me and the ones that made fun of me. However, in order for me to be obedient to the Lord and His Word, I knew that I must **forgive.** Matthew 18:21-22: *"Then came Peter to him and said Lord how oft shall my brothers sin against me, and I forgive him? till seven times? and Jesus saith unto him, I say not unto thee, until seven times; but until seventy times seven"* [endless]. As Mark 11:25-26 says, **Forgive!** As difficult as this may be, we must forgive in order for God to bless us as he wants to bless us. Many years ago we forgave all those people because of the love which God put in our heart. He never said it would be easy.

The love of God – John 3:16-18: ***"For God so loved the world*** [you and me] ***that he gave his only begotten son, that whosoever*** [including you and me] ***believeth in him should not perish, but have everlasting life. For God sent not his son into the world to condemn the world*** [man kind] ***but that the world through him might be saved. He that believeth on him is not condemned, but he that believeth not is condemned already, because he hath not believed in the name of the only begotten Son of God."***

Oh what love He must have to give us such a wonderful gift. Undeserving, unworthy as we are, regardless of our condition or situation, He will lift us up and make us someone fit for the kingdom of God, all because of His love, grace, and mercy. His love is not limited to time and space; He is omnipotent and omnipresent.

He can and will carry us beyond ourselves if only we will be obedient to His Word. He has not only provided us His Word but also has protected the Word through the centuries of time that you and I may know His will and way for our lives.

39

Prayer is another thing God has provided us that we may have direct contact to Him. We can call upon Him at any time, day or night. Psalm 55:16-17 *"As for me, I will call upon God and the Lord will save me. Evenings, mornings and at noon, will I pray and cry aloud, and he shall hear my voice."* Luke 18:1 *"Men ought always to pray and not to faint."* I have found answers to my questions as we prayed. Sometimes the answer came in the middle of the night, and sometimes it came through others. He may say yes, no, or wait. He knows best. He sees the whole picture and always does what is best for us. He only does things for two reasons, our good and His glory.

Sometimes I teach a lesson titled **When Does God Answer Prayer?** See Appendix A for seven answers.

This is the old home house I was born in. Virginia, Johnny, and Steven stand out front.

Chapter 8

My God Is Mighty!

My God is mighty, and He knows the path we take. It is great to know who is in control. God sees all things from the beginning to the end. He knows what is best for each one of us.

Of course we only see what is before us, and we act, or react accordingly. Sometimes we are prone to do whatever is convenient at the time. Thanks be unto Him, for He not only knows but also cares for us and sometimes in spite of ourselves. We see through a glass darkly even at our best, but if we put our trust in God by faith, then everything will work out fine.

So regardless of how hopeless life may seem from our view, God can and will take it and make something good if we will only trust in Him.

After joining the Gideons over twenty-five years ago, life has been more meaningful and rewarding. We have been able to reach out and place God's precious Word around the world. We have had a part in witnessing to others and directing them to the Lamb of God that takes away and forgives their sin. Oh what a wonderful blessing this has been.

In our church we were involved in many activities: teacher, Sunday school superintendent, deacon, youth leader and trainer, and some other leadership roles. Yet there seemed to be something else that the Lord had for us to do. When the Gideons invited us into the ministry, that void in our lives was filled.

We have been able to share with those in jail and prison by letting them know what the Lord could and would do for them if only they would accept Jesus Christ into their hearts and turn their lives over to Him. I love seeing families, spouses, children, anyone accepting Jesus as their Savior. Their lives will never be the same because **the hopelessness has changed to hope in just a matter of minutes.** Knowing this keeps me pushing on because it is all to the glory and honor of God.

We have the opportunity to share in many of our churches what mighty and wonderful things God is doing through this ministry. Our ministry's sole purpose (objective) is to win the lost to Jesus Christ. We not only give our time but also pay dues ourselves to cover the administrative cost and shipping so that one hundred percent of every cent that comes from our churches goes to print God's precious Word. We even provide the legs to get God's Word to where it is needed the most. For over one hundred and six years now, there has been an increase in funds and distributions each year. I do not know of any other association that can say that.

When fifteen of our members go and distribute 950,685 copies of God's Word in two weeks with the help of a few local Gideons in Columbia, South America, and over 74,000 people make professions of faith in Jesus Christ, this blesses my soul. (Seventy-four thousand and ninety-eight). We must be about our Father's business; the fruit of a Christian should be another Christian.

The Lord wants us to choose to serve Him. He could have made us as puppets, doing as He demanded, but that is not God's way. He made us as free moral agents. He gives us the choice to either accept Him and His will for our lives or to reject Him, His Son, and the salvation He has provided for everyone through Jesus Christ The Lord.

If we accept Him as our Savior and Lord, when this life is over, we shall spend eternity with Him in heaven, a place He has prepared for us. But if we reject Him, when this life is over, we will spend eternity in hell, a place prepared for the devil and all that reject Jesus Christ as their Savior. The Lord provided an escape for you and me when He took our sins upon Himself on the Cross of Calvary. He suffered our punishment and penalty; He took away the sting of death and the victory of the grave. By conquering death, hell, and the grave, He provided life for you and me. **Oh what a Savior!** He bought our pardon with His own life as if we had never sinned. **My hope is in nothing less than Jesus Christ and His righteousness.** I don't have any righteousness of my own.

Many of my life choices since coming to know my Lord have been directed by and through Him. Oh yes, some bad choices have been mine and mine alone. Sometimes we must confess that we have gotten and still do (sorry to say) get ahead of God's will. We think that we can do something ourselves but just end up making a mess.

There was one time in particular in 1960 when a couple of people said some things about me that were untrue. I got very upset and tried to take matters into my hands, which only made things worse. After nearly having a nervous breakdown, we learned quickly that we must let God handle the situation. From that day to now, we have learned to put all things in God's hands. The battle is the Lord's. II Chronicles 20:15 *"For the battle is not your's but God's."* God can take care of any and all of our needs. Sticks and stones may break our bones, but words can never harm us (only if we let them).

Of course God gives us the ability to do all that He asks us to do. Then, once we have done all we can with the strength, knowledge, and wisdom He has given us, we must leave the rest up to Him by faith. Hebrews 11:1 *"Faith is the substance of things hoped for, the evidence of things not seen."*

There are three things each of us should know about ourselves: where we have been (past), where we are (present), and where we are going (future).

With a very bad start in life, my mother dying at such a young age, not receiving the love and compassion that mothers usually give, being left on the porch of people who did not want us, enduring the terrible experiences of the county home, suffering the scars of being used and abused with no one around who really cared, being made fun of at school and other places, I was the scapegoat for others. This would leave me with a lot of hatred and bitterness inside my heart, but thanks to God, He gave me the ability to know the good from the bad and helped me to make the right choices. God sent some very special people into my life. **All that hopelessness changed into hope when He saved me by His marvelous grace from sin and myself.** That day I will never forget, for I have not been the same since. Though I have not been all that I could or should have been, I am so thankful that I am not what I once was.

With all of our failures through our disobedience and rebellion, God still loves us and draws us back unto Himself through the Holy Spirit as we repent of our sins. Thanks be unto Him for His mercy and grace. He carries us far beyond ourselves when we are obedient unto Him.

All of the achievements that have been accomplished in my life are because of Him and His blessings. My passing the G.E.D. Test with such good scores after being out of school for sixteen years had to be God giving me the understanding to do so. He gave me the ability to teach others and to give seminars in colleges and universities all over the United States. What a blessing it has been to work in the areas of job training and orientation training. Just being able to contribute to the welfare of others has been so satisfying. We have seen the smiles of so many that were not able to help themselves as we gave our spare time so they might have clothing to wear. We have had the privilege to tailor for very wealthy people, to work with celebrities from all walks of life and in so many different areas, to work with so many professionals, and to do all the special projects that presented challenges and rewards.

My family has been blessed so tremendously over and beyond our expectations. Since retiring from Blue Bell, my wife and I have been able to travel and see so much of this beautiful land that God has made for you and me. We have had the privilege of staying in some of the best motels and hotels, eating at some of the nicest restaurants, and meeting some of the nicest people, therefore making so many wonderful new friends. Only God could have carried us so far, and please remember that if He could do this for a poor boy like me, He can and will do it for you if you will only trust and let Him. Always please remember that **our hope** is in Jesus Christ and His righteousness. He can and will do even more than we can think or ask Him to do. **Let's keep our hope in Him and Him alone.**

It is important that we be consistent in our daily walk and talk. The only Bible some people read is the lives of us who are

Here I am at the monument made to Huckleberry Finn and Tom Sawyer at Hannibal, Missouri.

45

Virginia and Robert at Point Barrow, Alaska.

Christians. We must live so as not to turn them away from our Savior. God is the same today, yesterday, and forever more, never changing. It is important for us as his representatives and ambassadors to live a clean and trustworthy life so that others can read the same message each and every time they see us.

Virginia and I are standing at the 18th hole of Pebble Beach Golf Course, where we played in 2000.

Chapter 9

Continual Family Love

Regardless of time and distance, the love between my sister, my brothers, and me never ended. My love for each of them was and still is very strong. We surely would have loved to have been together growing up, but God knows best. We do not have any doubt about that.

Anne was the first of my siblings to pass away at the age of fifty-seven. She had a tough life, a life of abuse growing up with the family that the welfare had left her with. She married and had one daughter. Anne never came to grips with the problems of her youth; she just could not seem to let them go. I spoke to her many times and tried to counsel her. Her peace of mind would only last for a short time; then we would have to go through it again. I am so thankful for her love toward me.

Willie had a hard time forgetting his experiences in World War II where he was injured and left for dead by the enemy. He was shot down as he was hanging in the air. While still in service soon after returning stateside, Willie married Olivia, a wonderful lady, and they had one son. Olivia died at age fifty-seven, and Willie died at age seventy-one. Their son is a wonderful preacher, and their only grandson is also a minister. Thank God, there are those who are willing to tell the good news by preaching the Gospel of Christ.

Olivia Aheron (sister-in-law)

Jimmy and I are the only ones still living, but we are able to enjoy each other, and our families visit even though we live some distance apart. Jimmy was the brains of our family. He graduated from college and married a very smart and wonderful lady. Sondra was a teacher and a principal; she has many PH.D's. They have two children, one boy and one girl; both are highly intelligent. They both graduated from more than one university. Sondra helped me so much with my studies when I was taking night classes many years ago. Jimmy and Sondra do so much as volunteers with Hospice and American Red Cross. They are like God's angels to and for so many other people now that they are retired. What a wonderful world this would be if we had more like this family. I am so very thankful not only for my wife and family but also for any and all who have helped and encouraged me along the way.

May I share a few words of wisdom to those who just can't seem to turn their lives around? Please trust the Lord. The devil is so much bigger than we are. We are no match for old Lucifer the devil, but he is no match for my Lord. God says get thee behind me, and the devil flees. Greater is He that is in us than he that is in the world. We must also forgive. God says He will not forgive us if we do not forgive our fellowman. Hate, bitterness, animosity, jealousy,

Preachers Mark and John Mark, Willie and Olivia's son and grandson.

pride, envy, all will cause a defeated life in Christ Jesus. God is not pleased with a proud look. Give until it feels good. God loves a cheerful giver. We know that there are givers and takers. God gave us His Son (heaven's best); shouldn't we give our best! Smile and the whole world will smile at you. Love those that despitefully use or say things against you. It is easy for anyone to love those that return their love. But it takes the love and grace of God to love the enemy. Don't let situations or circumstances deter us from moving forward with our lives. Let's be that shining light in this dark world. The darker it is the brighter the light will be. Work as a servant and have a servant's heart. Labor while it is still day, for the night cometh when no man can work.

"The Lord is my Shepherd I shall not want" (Psalms 23:1); what a consolation. As one of His sheep, it blesses my soul that we know who is in control. *"Thy* [God's] *word is a lamp unto my feet and a light unto my path"* (Psalms 119:105). *"As far as the East is from the West, so far hath he removed our transgressions from us"* (Psalms 103:12). *"Bless the Lord, O my soul, and all that is within me, bless his holy name"* (Psalms 103:1). *"This poor man cried and the Lord heard him and saved him out of all his troubles. The angel of the Lord encampeth around about them that fear him, and delivereth them."* (Psalms 34:6-9)

"Oh taste and see the Lord is good; blessed is the man that trusteth in him. Oh fear the Lord, ye his saints; for there is no want to them that fear him." (Psalms 34:8,9)

"Fret not thyself because of evil doers, neither be thou envious against the workers of iniquity" (Psalms 37:1). *"Rest in the Lord and wait patiently for him. Fret not thyself because of him who prospereth in his way because of the man who bringeth wicked devices to pass"* (Psalms 37:7).

"Wait on the Lord and keep his way and he shall exalt thee to inherit the land; when the wicked are cut off, thou shalt see it" (Psalms 37:34).

"Mark the perfect [mature] *man and behold the upright; for the end of that man is peace"* (Psalms 37:37). *"And the peace of God which passeth all understanding shall keep your heart and minds through Jesus Christ"* (Philippians 4:7). The Apostle Paul says in Philippians 4:9 *"Those things, which ye have both learned, and received, and heard, and seen in me, do: and the God of peace shall be with you."*

A little earlier we mentioned fear. That is, we are to fear God only; Luke 12:4-5 *"and I say unto you my friends, be not afraid of them that kill the body, after that they have no more that they can do. But I will forewarn you whom ye shall fear. Fear him, which after he hath killed hath power to cast into hell; yea, I say unto you, fear him."*

The fear of man must be an awful thing. It robs people of so much. Faith can and will take its place if only we will let it. We do not have any fear of man. Thank God. Even the devil trembled at the command of God.

And as we think of the grace of God, and how He bestows His grace unto each of us, I am reminded of II Samuel 9:1-13 about Mephibosheth. That same grace has been mine to enjoy for a very long time, and it goes with each of us, each and every day. It is the amazing grace, and the marelous grace of God that sustains us. Thanks be unto God! We feast at the King's table as one of His children, just like Mephibosheth.

Virginia and I had this photo made while vacationing in Hawaii.

Chapter 10

Hope for the Hopeless

Hope for the hopeless is what this is all about. I John 4:11 *"Beloved, if God so loved us, we ought also to love one another."* The more a few people try to tear us down, the more the Lord lifts us up. What a wonderful, loving Lord we have. Oh, the green pastures he has provided with such peace and contentment. Psalms: 23:2-6 *"He maketh me to lie down in green pastures. He leadeth me beside the still waters. He restoreth my soul; he leadeth me in the paths of righteousness for his name's sake. Yea though I walk through the valley of the shadow of death, I will fear no evil; for thou art with me; thy rod and thy staff they comfort me. Thou preparest a table before me in the presence of mine enemies; thou anointest my head with oil; my cup runneth over. Surely goodness and mercy shall follow me all the days of my life; and I will dwell in the house of the Lord for ever."*

Just a short few years ago, I did go through the shadow of death, a couple of times. After going to several different doctors, one of them told me to set our house in order, for there was not anything they could do for me. An operation was out of the question. It would have been too risky, and the doctor would not take the chance. He stated that I might not be able to leave his office; that is how bad things were. I told the doctor not to worry or fret over it; it would not be anything he did or didn't do if I died in his office then or later. I told him that everything was totally in the Lord's hands. I had made all the preparations

51

necessary to face life or death if my Lord chose to take me home. I did not have any fear either way. The doctor looked at me and said that he had been practicing many years, but he had never had anyone to say that with such confidence and assurance. I told him that he had never had a John Robert Aheron before either. He agreed.

Another doctor recommended treatments. The first kind of treatment triggered a reaction to some medicine that another doctor prescribed. This caused major, life threatening problems. As I came close to death again, I lost fifty-one pounds and suffered liver damage. It took some time to diagnose the problem. I had to change the treatments to a new medicine. After one hundred treatments total, things are much better, and I have gained about twelve pounds back. I am feeling great and working hard. Most of my strength is back, and I am very active again.

Again, this health problem was a blessing in disguise. I needed to lose some weight and needed a different diet. It caused me to take another look at myself and where I was with our Lord. It made us live each day as though it was our last but plan for tomorrow as if tomorrow would come. We use our time as quality time, more for others. We have tried to adopt the title of the song – "Others" – as our motto. "Let us live for others that we may live like Thee." Two of our favorite hymns are "Blessed Assurance" and "How Great Thou Art."

"Blessed Assurance" was written by Fanny Crosby who was blind. It shows that we can know and have the assurance of our salvation. I John 5:13 *"These things have I written unto you that believe on the name of the Son of God; that ye may know that ye have eternal life, and that ye may believe on the name of the Son of God."*

"How Great Thou Art" describes the wonder and awesomeness of God. It has the idea that words will not adequately describe our Savior. John 21:25 *"And there are also many other things which Jesus did, the which, if they should be written every one, I suppose that even the world itself could not contain the books that should be written. Amen."*

"Jesus, Jesus, there's just something about that name." Keep your eyes upon Him, not me or others. He never fails. Trust Him. May God bless you and may the hope of God be with you forever. Hopefully you can now claim Colossians 1:27b, "...*Christ in you, the hope of glory.*" Also read Romans 5:1-21 (the entire chapter).

Romans 5:1-21:
1. *Therefore being justified by faith, we have peace with God through our Lord Jesus Christ:*
2. *By whom also we have access by faith into this grace wherein we stand, and rejoice in* **hope** *of the glory of God.*
3. *And not only so, but we glory in tribulations also: knowing that tribulation worketh patience;*
4. *And patience, experience; and experience,* **hope***:*
5. *And* **hope** *maketh not ashamed; because the love of God is shed abroad in our hearts by the Holy Ghost which is* **given** *unto us.*
6. *For when we were yet without strength, in due time Christ died for the ungodly.*
7. *For scarcely for a righteous man will one die: yet peradventure for a good man some would even dare to die.*
8. *But God* **commendeth** *his love toward us, in that, while we were yet sinners, Christ died for us.*
9. ***Much more*** *then, being now justified by his blood, we shall be saved from wrath through him.*
10. *For if, when we were enemies, we were reconciled to God by the death of his Son,* **much more***, being reconciled, we shall be saved by his life.*
11. *And not only so, but we also joy in God through our Lord Jesus Christ, by whom we have now received the atonement.*
12. *Wherefore, as by one man sin entered into the world, and death by sin; and so death passed upon all men, for that all have sinned:*

13. *(For until the law sin was in the world: but sin is not imputed when there is no law.*

14. *Nevertheless death reigned from Adam to Moses, even over them that had not sinned after the similitude of Adam's transgression, who is the figure of him that was to come.*

15. *But not as the offense, so also is the free **gift**. For if through the offense of one many be dead, **much more** the grace of God, and the **gift** by grace, which is by one man, Jesus Christ, hath abounded unto many.*

16. *And not as it was by one that sinned, so is the **gift**: for the judgment was by one to condemnation, but the free **gift** is of many offenses unto justification.*

17. *For if by one man's offense death reigned by one; **much more** they which receive abundance of grace and of the **gift** of righteousness shall reign in life by one, Jesus Christ.)*

18. *Therefore as by the offence of one judgment came upon all men to condemnation; even so by the righteousness of one the free **gift** came upon all men unto justification of life.*

19. *For as by one man's disobedience many were made sinners, so by the obedience of one shall many be made righteous.*

20. *Moreover the law entered, that the offense might abound. But where sin abounded, grace did **much more** abound:*

21. *That as sin hath reigned unto death, even so might grace reign through righteousness unto eternal life by Jesus Christ our Lord.*

There is **hope** for the **hopeless** and **much more** because of the **gift** (the free gift) God has given us through Jesus Christ our Lord. What joy, peace and love. It is so great to be forgiven, redeemed by the blood of the Crucified One.

Appendix A

WHEN DOES GOD ANSWER PRAYER?
(7 ANSWERS)

1 WHEN WE PRAY (ASK) IN JESUS NAME

John 14:13-15 And whatsoever ye shall ask in my name, that will I do, that the Father may be glorified in the Son.
14 If ye shall ask anything in my name, I will do *it*.
15 If ye love me, keep my commandments.

John 16:23-24 And in that day ye shall ask me nothing. Verily, verily, I say unto you, Whatsoever ye shall ask the Father in my name, he will give *it* you.
24 Hitherto have ye asked nothing in my name: ask, and ye shall receive, that your joy may be full.

NO OTHER NAME WILL WORK!

2 WHEN WE PRAY (ASK) ACCORDING TO HIS WILL

I John 5:14-15 And this is the confidence that we have in him, that, **if we ask anything according to his will, he heareth us:**
15 And if we know that he hear us, whatsoever we ask, we know that we have the petitions that we desired of him.

Matthew 6:8-13 Be not ye therefore like unto them: for your Father knoweth what things ye have need of before ye ask him.
9 After this manner therefore pray ye: Our Father which art in heaven, Hallowed be thy name.
10 Thy kingdom come. **Thy will be done in earth,** as *it is* in heaven.
11 Give us this day our daily bread.
12 And forgive us our debts, as we forgive our debtors.
13 And lead us not into temptation, but deliver us from evil: For thine is the kingdom, and the power, and the glory, for ever. Amen.

NOT OUR WILL!

Luke 11:1-4, 9, 10 And it came to pass, that, as he was praying in a certain place, when he ceased, one of his disciples said unto him, Lord, teach us to pray, as John also taught his disciples.

2 And he said unto them, When ye pray, say, Our Father which art in heaven, Hallowed be thy name. Thy kingdom come. **Thy will be done,** as in heaven, so in earth.

3 Give us day by day our daily bread.

4 And forgive us our sins; for we also forgive every one that is indebted to us. And lead us not into temptation; but deliver us from evil.

9 And I say unto you, ask, and it shall be given you; seek, and ye shall find; knock, and it shall be opened unto you.

10 For every one that asketh receiveth; and he that seeketh findeth; and to him that knocketh it shall be opened.

3 WHEN WE PRAY (ASK) WITH FAITH BELIEVING (TRUSTING)

Mark 11:22-24 And Jesus answering saith unto them, "Have faith in God.

23 For verily I say unto you, **That whosoever** shall say unto this mountain, 'Be thou removed, and be thou cast into the sea;' and shall not doubt in his heart, but **shall believe that those things which he saith shall come to pass; he shall have whatsoever he saith.**

24 Therefore I say unto you, **What things soever ye desire, when ye pray, believe that ye receive** *them*, **and ye shall have** *them*."

John 3:16-18 For God so loved the world, that he gave his only begotten Son, that whosoever believeth in him should not perish, but have everlasting life.

17 For God sent not his Son into the world to condemn the world; but that the world through him might be saved.

18 He that believeth on him is not condemned: but he that believeth not is condemned already, because he hath not believed in the name of the only begotten Son of God.

Romans 10:17 So then faith *cometh* by hearing, and hearing by the word of God.

Hebrews 11:6 But **without faith** *it is* **impossible to please** *him*: **for he that cometh to God must believe that he is, and** *that*

he is a rewarder of them that diligently seek him.

Romans 10:9-13 That if thou shalt confess with thy mouth the Lord Jesus, and shalt believe in thine heart that God hath raised him from the dead, thou shalt be saved.

10 For with the heart man believeth unto righteousness; and with the mouth confession is made unto salvation. For the scripture saith, Whosoever believeth on him shall not be ashamed.

12 For there is no difference between the Jew and the Greek: for the same Lord over all is rich unto all that call upon him.

13 For whosoever shall call upon the name of the Lord shall be saved.

4   WHEN WE ABIDE IN HIM AND HIS WORD ABIDES IN US

John 15:7 If ye abide in me, and my words abide in you, ye shall ask what ye will, and it shall be done unto you.

John 17:6-26 I have manifested thy name unto the men which thou gavest me out of the world: thine they were, and thou gavest them me; and they have kept thy word.

7   Now they have known that all things whatsoever thou hast given me are of thee.

8   For I have given unto them the words which thou gavest me; and they have received *them*, and have known surely that I came out from thee, and they have believed that thou didst send me.

9   I pray for them: I pray not for the world, but for them which thou hast given me; for they are thine. **[HE ONLY HEARS HIS CHILDREN EXCEPT A SINNER IN REPENTANCE.]**

10   And all mine are thine, and thine are mine; and I am glorified in them.

11   And now I am no more in the world, but these are in the world, and I come to thee. Holy Father, keep through thine own name those whom thou hast given me, that they may be one, as we *are*.

12   While I was with them in the world, I kept them in thy name: those that thou gavest me I have kept, and none of them is lost, but the son of perdition; that the scripture might be fulfilled.

13   And now come I to thee; and these things I speak in the world, that they might have my joy fulfilled in themselves.

14 I have given them thy word; and the world hath hated them, because they are not of the world, even as I am not of the world.

15 I pray not that thou shouldest take them out of the world, but that thou shouldest keep them from the evil.

16 They are not of the world, even as I am not of the world.

17 Sanctify them through thy truth: thy word is truth.

18 As thou hast sent me into the world, even so have I also sent them into the world.

19 And for their sakes I sanctify myself, that they also might be sanctified through the truth.

20 Neither pray I for these alone, but for them also which shall believe on me through their word;

21 That they all may be one; as thou, Father, *art* in me, and I in thee, that they also may be one in us: that the world may believe that thou hast sent me.

22 And the glory which thou gavest me I have given them; that they may be one, even as we are one:

23 **I in them,** and **thou in me,** that they may be made perfect in one; and that the world may know that thou hast sent me, and hast loved them, as thou hast loved me.

24 Father, I will that they also, whom thou hast given me, be with me where I am; that they may behold my glory, which thou hast given me: for thou lovedst me before the foundation of the world.

25 O righteous Father, the world hath not known thee: but I have known thee, and these have known that thou hast sent me.

26 And I have declared unto them thy name, and will declare *it*: that the love wherewith thou hast loved me may be in them, and I in them.

5   WHEN WE PRAY (ASK) WITH HUMILITY

II Chronicles 7:14 If my people, which are called by my name, **shall humble themselves, and pray,** and seek my face, and turn from their wicked ways; **then will I hear from heaven,** and will forgive their sin, and will heal their land.

Luke 18:9-14 And he spake this parable unto certain which trusted in themselves that they were righteous, and despised others:

10 Two men went up into the temple to pray; the one a Pharisee, and the other a publican.

11 The Pharisee stood and prayed thus with himself, God, I thank thee, that I am not as other men *are*, extortioners, unjust, adulterers, or even as this publican.

12 I fast twice in the week, I give tithes of all that I possess.

13 And the publican, standing afar off, would not lift up so much as *his* eyes unto heaven, but smote upon his breast, saying, God be merciful to me a sinner.

14 I tell you, this man went down to his house justified *rather* than the other: for every one that exalteth himself shall be abased; and **he that humbleth himself shall be exalted.**

Luke 18:1 And he spake a parable unto them *to this end*, that men ought always to pray, and not to faint;

I Peter 5:6-7 Humble yourselves therefore under the mighty hand of God, that he may exalt you in due time:

7 **Casting all your care upon him; for he careth for you.**

James 4:3-10 Ye ask, and receive not, because ye ask amiss, that ye may consume *it* upon your lusts.

4 Ye adulterers and adulteresses, know ye not that the friendship of the world is enmity with God? Whosoever therefore will be a friend of the world is the enemy of God.

5 Do ye think that the scripture saith in vain, The spirit that dwelleth in us lusteth to envy?

6 But he giveth more grace. Wherefore he saith, God resisteth the proud, but giveth grace unto the humble.

7 Submit yourselves therefore to God. Resist the devil, and he will flee from you.

8 Draw nigh to God, and he will draw nigh to you. Cleanse *your* hands, *ye* sinners; and purify *your* hearts, *ye* double minded.

9 Be afflicted, and mourn, and weep: let your laughter be turned to mourning, and *your* joy to heaviness.

10 Humble yourselves in the sight of the Lord, and he shall lift you up.

Ephesians 3:14 For this cause I bow my knees unto the Father of our Lord Jesus Christ,

6   WHEN WE ARE OBEDIENT TO HIS WORD

I John 3:22 And **whatsoever we ask, we receive of him, because we keep his commandments, and do those things**

that are pleasing in his sight.

John 14:15 If ye love me, keep my commandments.

Psalms 66:18-20 If I regard iniquity in my heart, the Lord will not hear *me*:
19 *But* verily God hath heard *me*; he hath attended to the voice of my prayer.
20 Blessed *be* God, which hath not turned away my prayer, nor his mercy from me.

Mark 11:25-26 And when ye stand praying, <u>forgive</u>, if ye have ought against any: that your Father also which is in heaven may forgive you your trespasses.
26 **But if ye do not <u>forgive</u>, neither will your Father which is in heaven forgive your trespasses.**

I John 1:9 If we confess our sins, he is faithful and just to forgive us *our* sins, and to cleanse us from all unrighteousness.

Matthew 5:44 But **I say unto you, Love your enemies, bless them that curse you, do good to them that hate you,** and **pray for them which despitefully use you, and persecute you; [THIS IS NOT EASY BUT WE MUST DO IT IN ORDER TO HAVE OUR PRAYERS ANSWERED.]**

7 **WHEN HE WANTS TO AND WHEN IT PLEASES HIM**

Psalms 115:3 But our God *is* in the heavens: **he hath done whatsoever he hath pleased.**

Psalms 135:5-6 For I know that the LORD *is* great, and *that* our Lord *is* above all gods.
6 **Whatsoever the LORD pleased, <u>*that*</u> did he in heaven, and in earth, in the seas, and all deep places.**

Romans 9:15-16 For he saith to Moses, **I will have mercy on whom I will have mercy,** and **I will have compassion on whom I will have compassion.**
16 So then *it is* not of him that willeth, nor of him that runneth, but of **God that sheweth mercy.**

ORDER FORM

Copies of this book may be ordered directly from the author. The following prices apply:

Retail $3.95 _____

Add 7% sales tax for NC residents _____

Shipping/handling
$2.00 for one or two books _____
$1.00 for each additional book _____

TOTAL AMOUNT: _____

To order books, send a check or money order to:

Robert Aheron
530 Ogburn Mill Road
Stokesdale, NC 27357
(336) 643-4206

With all orders, include the following:

Name _____

Address_____

Phone Number _____